Curriculum Visions

Hindu art and writing

Glossary

AARTI A type of prayer in which light, in the form of burning candles, incense and other items are offered as a thanks in worship to God.

DURGA A form of the goddess Parvati, who is the wife of Lord Shiva. She protects people from evil and misery.

GANESHA The elephant-headed son of the god Shiva and the goddess Parvati, and the god of wisdom.

GODS AND GODDESSES Hindus believe in one God, but they believe that God has many different forms, or parts, called gods and goddesses and that worshipping any god or goddess is the same as worshipping God.

HINDU A person who follows the Hindu faith. Hindus believe many different things, but all Hindus believe in one God, but that God can be shown in many different ways.

HOLY BOOKS Books of religious teachings and stories. There are many different Hindu scriptures. The two main groups are shruti, believed to have come directly from God, and smitri, which were composed long ago by scholars and poets.

HYMN A religious song or a song with a religious meaning.

KALI Another form or part of the goddess Lakshmi. But Kali is the part of Lakshmi that destroys evil and demons.

KRISHNA A form of the god Vishnu. Krishna stands for joy, freedom and love.

LAKSHMI The wife of Lord Vishnu and the goddess of wealth, beauty and good luck.

LORD Another name for God.

MURTI A sacred statue of a god or goddess. The statues do not only stand for the god or goddess, but Hindus believe that the gods and goddesses are present in the statues during worship.

OFFERING A gift left for a god or goddess. Almost anything can be an offering, such as food, prayers or song. Hindus believe that the gods bless the offerings and the giver.

PUJA Worship in Hinduism. There are many different types of puja, but they usually involve spoken prayers, hymns, seeing the gods and goddesses and making offerings to the gods and goddesses.

RAMA AND SITA Lord Rama is a part of the god Vishnu and the prince of the kingdom of Ayodhya, and Sita is his wife.

RAMAYANA A story which is also part of Hindu holy scripture. It tells the story of Lord Rama and his wife Sita. In the Ramayana are instructions and advice telling people the correct ways to behave and to worship.

RANGOLI A design made from coloured sand or grains of rice. The designs are made in doorways and other places as a way to celebrate festivals.

SANSKRIT A language used in ancient India. Hindu holy books are written in Sanskrit.

SHRINE Each murti is placed in a shrine, which can be a simple box or a whole room. The shrine is a home for the murti, and so for the god or goddess.

SYMBOL An object, image, picture or letter that has a special meaning. Some symbols can have more than one meaning.

TILAKA Also called bindi or chandlo, these are marks made from scented paste, ash or coloured powders that are reminders that God is always with each worshipper.

VEHICLE A symbol, usually an animal, that is shown with the god or goddess in paintings and statues. The vehicle is a reminder of an important aspect of the god or goddess.

Contents

As you go through the book, look for words in **BOLD CAPITALS**. These words are defined in the glossary.

⚠ Understanding others

Remember that other people's beliefs are important to them. You must always be considerate and understanding when studying about faith.

Hindu worship through art

Art is an important part of the Hindu faith.

People show their faith in many ways, for example, through prayer. But there are many other ways that people can express their faith.

Art is anything that people create in order to express ideas, thoughts or feelings. Many people show their faith through arts such as painting, sculpture, drama or music. These arts can help us feel a certain way, such as happy or sad. They can also remind us of important things and teach us stories and ideas. Many religions also use words and symbols to help teach important ideas.

For example, worshippers may sing songs which make them feel joyous and happy as part of worship.

Hindus worship in many different ways, and Hindu worship involves using all of the senses. So, many types of art are used during worship and in everyday life to show their faith.

Paintings and statues of the gods and goddesses are a focus for worship, and help Hindus feel closer to God. Paintings and drawings are used to illustrate stories from the Hindu holy books. Music and drama help bring religious feelings and stories to life.

Many Hindus decorate their homes
and workplaces with symbols and
other types of art that have religious
meaning. In this way they can bring
God into everyday life.

The colours, words and
symbols used in these arts all help
worshippers express their faith in
different ways.

As you read through this book,
you will have a chance to explore
many of the different ways that
Hindus use the arts in the practice
of their faith.

▼ A decoration hanging on a house
wall showing Ganesha inside the
Aum, or Om, symbol (see page 6).

Symbols in Hindu art

Special symbols can add meaning to Hindu works of art.

A symbol is a design, drawing or object that can have many different meanings. Many of the symbols used in Hinduism stand for God.

Why do Hindus use so many symbols?

Hindus believe that God is everywhere. Because Hinduism is an ancient religion, over time a large number of symbols have begun to be used to stand for God. Some of these symbols are used during worship services and others are used to remind people of gods and goddesses. On these pages you can see some of these symbols and find out what they stand for.

Aum

The symbol Aum is also written Om, and is sometimes called pranava. It is actually a sound that is made up of three syllables, aa, au and ma, that are spoken together to make one long sound which sounds like "aaaauuummm". Aum is spoken at the beginning of many prayers.

The symbol for the sound can be seen in every Hindu temple and shrine. Hindu tradition says that God created the Universe by making this sound. So, the Aum symbol stands for God and for the entire Universe. It is one of the most important symbols in Hinduism.

▲ Swastika symbol on a purnakumbha.

Swastika

This symbol is in the shape of a cross with branches bent at right angles and facing in a clockwise direction. The branches point in all four directions and stand for the way that God is everywhere. It is also a symbol for good luck and protection.

The word 'Swastika' is an ancient word in the Sanskrit language. It means "Good will win". So, the symbol also stands for the belief that good thoughts and actions will always defeat evil thoughts and actions.

The lotus

This flower grows with its roots in the mud. It sends a long stem up through the water and the flower stands above the water. The lotus grows in mud but it is beautiful and the flower rests above the water but does not touch it. So, the lotus stands for the good that is inside everyone and the way that anyone can rise up to be with God. The lotus also stands for the beginning of the world.

▼ The Aum symbol inside a lotus flower design.

The purnakumbha

The word purnakumbha means a 'full pitcher' and a purnakumbha is an earthen pot or pitcher which is full of water and fresh mango leaves, and has a coconut on top. During worship, the pitcher is placed next to a shrine or next to an image of a god or goddess. The pot stands for Mother Earth, the water and leaves stand for life and the coconut stands for God. The pitcher may also stand for the goddess Lakshmi.

Fruits and leaves

Some other natural objects that stand for God are fruits, milk, betel leaves, betel-nuts, banyan leaves, and bel leaves. These things may be placed on a shrine during worship.

Lingam and yoni

Sometimes a stone called a lingam is used to stand for Lord Shiva. The stone may be placed in a stand called a yoni. Together, the lingam and yoni stand for nature and the creation of new life. During worship, offerings of milk or of water may be poured over the lingam and yoni.

Conch shell

The conch shell may be blown during worship. The god Vishnu is usually shown holding a conch shell that stands for the belief that life began in the water. In Hindu holy stories, ancient Indian warriors would blow conch shells to announce battles. So the conch shell can also stand for the way that good will defeat evil. The sound may be a reminder for everyone to 'wake up' and defeat evil thoughts and actions.

Dipa Lamps

Dipa lamps are often made from clay and are used during worship and during the holiday of Diwali. They stand for the way that the light of knowledge and of God defeats the darkness of ignorance and evil.

During Diwali the lamps are lit to welcome Lakshmi, the goddess of wealth, into people's homes. They are also reminders of the story of Rama and Sita, which is told during Diwali. In this story, Lord Rama and his wife Sita return home to their kingdom after a 14-year exile and the people of their kingdom lit thousands of clay lamps to welcome them back home.

The lamps burn ghee (made from butter) and may have one, three or five wicks. During worship the lighted lamps are waved in front of the gods and goddesses as an offering. The gods bless the light and then worshippers wave their own hands over the flames so they can share the blessing.

▲ The god Vishnu is often shown carrying a conch shell in one of his hands.

▼ Cows are reminders of Lord Krishna.

Cow

Cows stand for life, non-violence and purity. In ancient times, farmers and other people relied on cows for many things. Cows give milk to drink and to be made into cheese and butter. Bulls were used to plough the fields so crops could be sown, and their manure was used to grow the crops so there was food to eat. Hindus do not worship cows, but they are a reminder of life. They are also a reminder of Lord Krishna, who was a cowherd as a boy.

Bull and trident

A bull accompanies the god Shiva, so some Hindus use a bull as a symbol of Lord Shiva. You may see a drawing or painting of a bull on temples that are dedicated to worshipping Lord Shiva. Some Hindus believe that the bull stands for justice. The three-headed spear, or trident, is a weapon that is carried by Lord Shiva and by the goddess Shakti.

▶ The bull is a reminder of Lord Shiva.

◀ The trident is a reminder of Lord Shiva and of the goddess Shakti.

▼ This yantra is called the shree yantra – it can stand for the goddess Lakshmi.

Yantra

Some Hindu traditions use designs called yantras to represent gods and goddesses and God. One of the most popular is called the shree yantra, which stands for the goddess Lakshmi. The shree yantra is made up of triangles. The design helps worshippers to concentrate on God.

9

Symbols used in worship

Many symbols are also used in Hindu worship as reminders of different parts of God.

Hindus use different items to help them use all of their senses during worship. Worshipping with all your senses is one way to show that every part of the person is worshipping. Here are some items and symbols that are used during worship.

Incense

Worshippers light an incense stick and move it around the shrine in circles. This purifies the air and brings a pleasing aroma to the shrine for the gods.

Kum kum powder

Worshippers will make a paste out of the red kum kum powder. They use this to make a mark on the forehead of the images. This is again a sign of respect and devotion to the gods. They will also make a mark on their own forehead as a sign that God has blessed them.

Bell

Worshippers ring the bell to let God know that they have come to worship and to invite God into the temple or home.

Food and flowers

Worshippers offer food and flowers at the shrine for the gods to bless. This blessed food is called 'prashad'. It is later eaten by the worshippers.

Container of water and a spoon

Worshippers offer water to the gods and goddesses on a spoon. This is to show respect to the gods. Traditionally in India, people welcome a guest into the house by offering them water to drink and to wash. At the start of the day, the mother of the household will wash the murtis – again to show devotion and respect to them.

Lamp

Worshippers light a lamp and move it around in circles to bring light to the shrine. This light is a symbol of God's presence. The lamps used are often made of a metal, such as brass, and have three or five wicks.

▲▶ (Top) A Hindu priest waves a lamp in a shrine during aarti. (Right) This boy is receiving God's blessing during aarti.

Symbols used during aarti

The Aarti ceremony is a part of Hindu worship (puja) when worshippers make offerings to God in order to show their love for God. A number of symbols are used during aarti. These stand for the five elements from which everything is made, according to the Hindu tradition.

A conch shell is blown at the beginning of the ceremony. This stands for space and for the Universe. Then incense and flowers are offered. They stand for the Earth. Then a fan is waved. This stands for air.

The aarti lamp stands for the fifth element, fire. During the service, the lamp is moved in a circular, clockwise motion in front of the shrines of the gods while a prayer is recited. The aarti lamp is then taken round the worshippers who hold their hands over the flames and then pass them over their forehead and hair. This stands for receiving God's blessing. The circular motion of the lamp stands for the cycle of life.

Showing faith by wearing symbols

Many Hindus wear temporary marks on their foreheads as a sign of their faith.

During and after worship, many Hindus wear marks on their foreheads made out of coloured powder. These marks are called tilaka, bindi or chandlo and they are a reminder that God is always present. There are many different shapes of tilaka and each shape stands for something different.

The tilaka is a type of decoration, but it is also an identifying mark. It shows which Hindu tradition a worshipper follows, and which gods or goddesses a person worships.

▲ This elephant is painted with a tilaka that stands for Shiva.

◀▶ These worshippers are wearing the tilaka that stands for Vishnu.

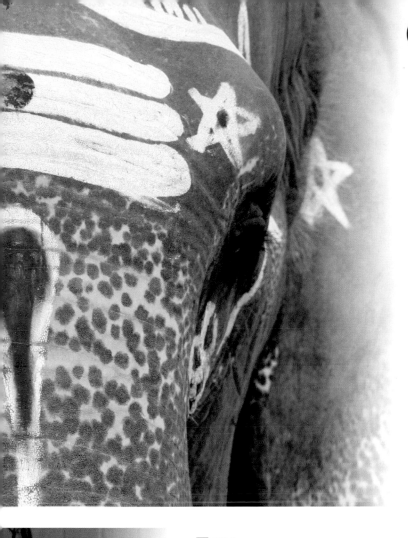

▼ This woman wears a simple red dot to show her Hindu faith.

The powder or paste that is used to make the tilaka is first presented during worship so that it can be blessed by God.

The tilaka is usually placed on the forehead between the eyebrows. This spot is sometimes called the 'third eye' and is a reminder that God sees everything and is with us all the time.

Different types of tilaka

People who worship Shiva may wear a tilaka of three horizontal lines made out of ashes.

People who worship Vishnu use clay (sometimes gathered from holy rivers) or sandalwood paste to make a U-shape. This stands for the heel of Lord Vishnu.

People who worship Devi use a red powder called kum kum, or red turmeric to make a vertical line or dot.

Many Hindus wear a mark called a tilaka chandlo. It consists of a U-shape made from yellow sandalwood paste with a dot (chandlo), made from red powder, in the centre. For some, the yellow U-shape stands for God and the red dot stands for the worshipper. For others, the U-shape stands for the idea of looking upward, to the heavens, while the red dot stands for Lakshmi, the goddess of prosperity.

Some people wear a simple red dot (a chandlo) as a reminder of their faith.

Representing gods and goddesses

Pictures or statues of gods and goddesses are important in Hindu worship.

During worship, Hindus use pictures, statues and drawings of the gods and goddesses. These images are called murtis.

The pictures and statues help worshippers to think about the gods and goddesses and to remember what they stand for. Most Hindus believe that, during worship, the gods and goddesses enter the murtis and are present for the worship service.

A picture or statue does not become a murti unless special prayers are said when it is placed in the temple or home. After this, it becomes a focus for worship.

The murti may be made of different materials, such as wood, stone, paper, or metal, and they are usually placed in a shrine.

The shrine looks a bit like a house, palace or temple. This is because it is a house for the gods and goddesses. The shrine is usually decorated with furniture, flowers, lights or other nice things that you might find in a house or palace. Making the shrine look attractive is important, because it is a way of showing love and devotion to the gods and goddesses.

What the murtis tell us

The things shown in each picture or statue tell us all about the god or goddess shown. For example, Lakshmi is often shown with gold coins. This tells us that she is the goddess of wealth.

In the pictures or statues, the gods and goddesses are usually shown with a bird or an animal, called a 'vehicle'. The vehicle also tells us something about the god. For example, pictures of the god Brahma usually show him with a swan or goose. The swan and the goose stand for knowledge, so showing them next to Brahma is a reminder that he is the god of religious knowledge.

You can tell a great deal about the gods and goddesses by looking at their images and the things in their shrines. On the following pages you will see some images of the most popular gods and goddesses, and learn what they tell worshippers.

◀ A murti in a Hindu temple.

▼ A statue of the god Shiva with a cobra, which stands for Shiva's ability to destroy evil and (below right) a statue of Shiva as Lord of the Dance.

Shiva

Lord Shiva is the god of mercy and compassion. He protects worshippers from evil forces such as ignorance, greed and anger. He destroys ignorance, and helps worshippers to become wise. Most of the symbols that are shown with Shiva are reminders that Shiva is very kind and brings good luck.

Shiva is sometimes shown with a blue throat. This is a reminder of a story in the Hindu holy books of how Shiva once drank a poison that would have destroyed the world.

Shiva is often shown with four arms, which stand for his superhuman power to do many things at the same time. He carries a three-pronged weapon called a trident, which he uses to destroy evil and which is a reminder that he helps with three different things – creation, destruction and preservation. He holds a drum whose sound creates life. His prayer beads stand for time (past, present and future). He is also often shown with a third eye, which stands for his ability to see how people behave and act.

Shiva is often shown with a cobra, the Naga, wrapped around his neck. The cobra is a symbol of fertility and strength. The water flowing from his hair stands for the River Ganges.

The three horizontal lines on his forehead may stand for the three sources of light – fire, Sun and Moon; or his ability to see the past, present and future. Shiva is often shown sitting on a tiger skin, which stands for the way that he can control the strong forces of nature. Shiva's vehicle is a white bull, which stands for strength. By riding the bull, Shiva is shown to be in control of strong forces that can cause harm, such as anger and hatred. When he is riding the bull, he sits in the pose used for meditation, which shows that Shiva is calm and in control.

One common image of Shiva is called 'Lord of the Dance'. In these pictures Shiva holds a small drum, which controls the rhythm of creation, and there is a flame behind him, which stands for destruction. He offers protection and blessing with his lower right hand, and his raised left foot stands for salvation. The figure under Shiva's right foot is a demon that stands for forgetfulness and ignorance.

▼ A statue of Brahma showing him with four heads and four arms.

Brahma

Brahma stands for the creation of the world. He is shown with four heads and four arms that stand for the four points of the compass. He may be shown holding a vase of water, which stands for the creation of the universe, a rosary for counting the passage of time, a spoon used by ancient priests when they made sacrifices to God, and the four Vedas, the ancient sacred books of the Hindus.

He is sometimes shown with a discus and an alms bowl. He may be shown sitting on a lotus throne. He is often bearded, and may wear a black or white garment.

His wife is Saraswati, goddess of wisdom and music, and his vehicle is a swan or a goose.

Vishnu

Whenever evil gets the upper hand, Vishnu comes to Earth in a form called an avatar and restores the balance. The most important avatars are Krishna and Rama.

Because he is responsible for stability and order, Vishnu is also the god of home and family.

Vishnu is shown with either two or four arms. When shown with four arms, these stand for his power over both the four points of the compass and the four stages of life. Sometimes his fourth hand is raised in the traditional hand gesture that means protection. Images of Vishnu try to combine compassion and strength.

Vishnu carries four symbols. The discus and club are both weapons, which stand for his ability to destroy evil and ignorance. The lotus stands for fertility and rebirth. The conch shell is blown in India like a trumpet during many sacred rituals. It stands for purity and goodness.

Vishnu's vehicle is Garuda, a bird with a man's head.

Vishnu is often shown with blue skin, which may stand for the sky and the ocean.

▼ A painting of Vishnu.

Sita

Rama

Hanuman

Rama and Sita

Rama is the seventh avatar of Vishnu and Sita is his wife and an avatar of the goddess Lakshmi. The Ramayana, which is one of the most popular stories in the Hindu tradition, tells the story of Rama's life. The story tells of how he was cheated of his rightful role as king and is banished to the forest where Sita is kidnapped by the evil Ravana. Helped by Hanuman, the god-king of the monkeys, Rama eventually defeats Ravana and his army in battle and rescues Sita. They then return to their kingdom where Rama is given his rightful place as king.

Rama is an example of reason, doing the right thing and virtue. He is often shown wearing a tall, cone-shaped cap which stands for his role as king.

Rama is an example of the perfect son, husband and king, while Sita is an example of the perfect daughter, wife and queen.

Hanuman

Hanuman is usually shown as part of the story of the Ramayana. In the story, Hanuman saves the life of Sita, Lord Rama's wife, and also of Lakshmana, Lord Rama's brother. Images of Hanuman often show him holding a mountain in his hand as a reminder of how he saved Lakshmana when he was wounded. Hanuman was sent to fetch healing herbs which grew on a particular mountain. He didn't know which herbs to pick, so he picked up the whole mountain and brought it back.

Hanuman is often shown with his paws closed together as in prayer. This is a reminder of Hanuman's devotion to God and a reminder that animals were also created by God.

Krishna

Krishna

Krishna is the eighth avatar of Vishnu, and he is worshipped by more Hindus than any other form of Vishnu. Krishna stands for joy, freedom and love. In his adult life, Krishna was the wise hero of the ancient epic the Mahabharata, where he gave the basic ideas of Hinduism.

Some images show him dancing and playing his flute to cow herds (he spent time as a cow herd when he was young). He is also shown defeating evil, for example, destroying the evil snake, Kaliya, who had poisoned the waters of one of India's sacred rivers.

As an adult, he is usually shown with blue-black skin, wearing a yellow loincloth and a crown of peacock feathers. He may also be shown as a mischievous child or a baby. There are many stories in the Hindu scriptures telling about his childhood.

Kali

Lakshmi (see page 21)

Lakshmi is the goddess of fortune and wealth and the wife of Vishnu.

As the goddess of good fortune she is shown with four arms. Two of her hands hold lotus flowers and a third pours out wealth in the form of gold coins. Her fourth hand is held out in the gesture of blessing. But she is also the goddess of beauty and so she is also shown as a young and beautiful goddess decorated with jewels and with only two arms.

She is often shown seated on a lotus, being showered by two elephants who are pouring pots of water over her head. The lotus stands for wealth and prosperity, because crops need water to grow.

Lakshmi's vehicle is a white owl. Because the owl hunts at night, it is a reminder that it takes hard work at all times to be prosperous.

Because Lakshmi brings good luck and prosperity, her image is often displayed in homes or over doorways, so that she can bring happiness and good luck to everyone in the house.

Kali

Kali is the destroyer of evil and of demons and so her image is very frightening. Kali stands for the frightening, painful side of life which must be overcome before we can be closer to God. She is also a reminder of death, which is a part of life.

She is usually shown naked or wearing a tiger skin, with tangled hair and rolling eyes. She has fang-like teeth, and her large tongue drips with blood and hangs from her mouth. She wears a necklace of skulls.

She is usually shown with four arms, two of which hold severed heads while the other two hold a dagger and a sword. In some images she also holds a rope and is standing on Shiva.

Her hands are blood stained, but one is often raised in a gesture of protection. This is a reminder that God looks over the dead as well as the living.

Ganesha

Ganesha

Ganesha is the god who removes barriers or obstacles to happiness and brings wisdom and good fortune. He is also worshipped at the beginning of any new venture, such as a wedding, starting a school year or building a new house. Ganesha is often shown with an open hand, palms upturned. Sometimes he is shown holding a gift, which is a reminder that he grants favours to his worshippers.

Because Ganesha is also the god of wisdom and learning, you can find a picture of him at the beginning of some books. He may be shown holding a tusk to use as a pen.

Ganesha is the son of Shiva and Parvati. Statues of him are placed in doorways as a reminder of how he defended his mother shortly after she created him.

Ganesha has an elephant's head and a human body with a pot belly. The elephant's head stands for gaining knowledge by listening (ears) and thinking (large head). The two tusks, one whole and the other broken, stand for the way that the world has both perfect things and imperfect things in it. Ganesha's pot belly may be a reminder of an ability to digest whatever experiences life brings. Ganesha has one leg on the ground and the other one folded as if he were meditating. This stands for the balance between everyday life and religious life.

In his hands Ganesha holds a rope, to trap things which distract us, and a goad, to help push us along the path of wisdom.

Ganesha loves sweets – his favourite is called a ladoo – and he is often shown holding a sweet as a symbol of prosperity and well-being.

He is pictured with four arms as reminders of the four holy books called the Vedas. His vehicle is a rat or a mouse because rats and mice are known for their ability to gnaw through barriers. The combination of the elephant and the rat or mouse is a reminder that all obstacles to happiness, big and small, can be removed.

Durga

Durga is also called the Mother Goddess, or Divine Mother, and she has many forms. Durga protects humans from evil and misery by destroying evil forces such as selfishness, jealousy, prejudice, hatred and anger.

One story of Durga's birth says that she was born, fully grown, from flames that came out from the mouths of the gods, so that she could destroy the buffalo demon, a symbol of death.

Durga is often shown with eight arms, which may stand for health, education, wealth, organisation, unity, fame, courage and truth. Other images show Durga with ten arms. Her vehicle is a lion or tiger which is a reminder that she is strong and can destroy evil.

Other reminders of her strength include weapons, such as a trident, a discus, a bow and arrow, a sword and shield, and a javelin. These stand for the destruction of evil and the protection of good.

Durga

Learning about faith through stories

Stories about the gods and goddesses help teach people how to worship and how to treat others.

The Hindu holy books tell many stories about gods and goddesses, kings and queens, wise men and ordinary people. These stories all help to teach people the proper way to worship and to behave. They also help people understand the ideals of Hinduism and to understand and overcome any hardships life brings.

Two of the most important stories in Hinduism are the Ramayana and the Mahabharata. Both of these stories are very long and have many characters.

The Mahabharata tells the story of Lord Krishna, the eighth avatar of Lord Vishnu. The main story tells of a struggle between two groups of cousins, the Kauravas and the Pandavas. At the end is a great battle that is won by the heroes – the Pandavas. One section of the Mahabharata, called the Bhagvad Gita, is a long discussion about the proper way to live life.

The Ramayana is one of the most popular stories in Hinduism. It tells the story of the life of Lord Rama of Ayodhya, the seventh avatar of Lord Vishnu. The Ramayana is more than just an interesting story. Woven into the story are teachings about the correct way for kings to behave to their subjects, how husbands and wives should treat each other, and how to be faithful to our family and those we love. The story teaches many lessons about how good behaviour leads to peace and harmony for everyone, while bad behaviour causes misery. You can see this by reading a short version of part of the story on the following pages. As you read, try to think about what lessons the story is teaching.

There are hundreds of other stories in Hinduism that tell about the lives of the gods and goddesses. For example, one popular story tells about the birth of the goddess Lakshmi. You can read a version of this story opposite.

▶ **The goddess Lakshmi is shown sitting on a lotus flower.**

The birth of Lakshmi

Durvasa was a wise man with a very short temper. One day he gave Indra, the king of the gods, a garland of flowers that would never wilt. Indra gave this garland to his elephant, Airavata.

One day Durvasa saw the elephant trampling the divine garland and, because he was short-tempered, he cursed Indra for showing him disrespect. Durvasa's curse was that Indra and all the gods would lose their power because they were so proud and vain. The demons heard this curse and took away all their powers and sent all the gods out of the heavens.

The defeated gods then went to the creator god, Lord Brahma, and asked him what to do. Lord Brahma told the gods that they could have their powers back if they churned the ocean of milk. Instead of butter, the ocean would turn into a nectar which would give the gods back their powers.

The gods then went to Lord Vishnu to seek his help with their task. Lord Vishnu used the king of the serpents, Vasuki, as a rod and all the gods took a turn to churn the ocean of milk.

As the gods churned, many divine gifts came out of the ocean of milk. One of these gifts was Lakshmi. Because of this, Lakshmi is also called the daughter of the sea; the Moon also appeared from the ocean during the churning, and so the Moon is called Lakshmi's brother.

Weblink: www.CurriculumVisions.com

The Ramayana

Here is a very short version of a part of the Ramayana.

King Dasharatha of Ayodhya had three wives and four sons. When the princes reached adulthood it was felt that they should marry.

At that time, King Janaka of Mithila had four beautiful daughters. Among these, Sita was the most pure, graceful, modest and beautiful. King Janaka had agreed that Sita could marry any prince she wanted, as long as he could perform a great feat – bending and stringing the Bow of Shiva. The bow of Lord Shiva was huge, and it could not be bent and strung by anyone who was selfish, dishonest or cowardly.

Princes from all over India, including Rama and his brothers, travelled to Mithila to try to win the hand of Sita. One by one, each prince tried to lift, bend and string the bow of Shiva. But even the most powerful of all the kings, the great Ravana of Lanka, could not even move the bow one inch above the ground! Everyone laughed at Ravana's defeat and made him feel ashamed.

At last it was the turn of Rama. Rama first saluted the bow and prayed to Shiva to give him strength and courage. Then Rama was able to lift, bend and string the bow. The whole royal court was filled with shouts of 'Glory Unto Rama, Victory to Rama'. This made King Ravana jealous and he vowed to get even with Rama one day.

So Rama got married to Sita, and his brothers got married to Sita's sisters.

After many years, King Dasharatha decided that it was time to give his kingdom to his beloved son Rama. A long time before, the king's third and youngest wife, Kaikeyi, had saved the King's life, and as a reward he had promised to grant her two wishes. Now, Kaikeyi's evil maid servant suggested to Kaikeyi that she should use one of the wishes to make her son Bharat, king.

So Kaikeyi asked King Dasharatha to banish Rama from the kingdom for 14 years, and to place Bharat on the throne instead. The King was shocked, and his heart was broken, but he knew that he had to keep his promise to his wife. So Rama went to exile happily, knowing that to obey and serve his father was the highest duty of a son.

Soon after Rama left for the forest, King Dasharatha died and Bharat went to the forest to ask Rama to come back to Ayodhya. But Rama had promised his father that he would leave Ayodhya for 14 years and he would not break his promise. So Rama refused to return. When he heard this, Bharat took Rama's wooden sandals and placed them on Ayodhya's throne. Bharat promised that, until his brother returned from exile, he would serve the kingdom as a true and honest ruler in his place.

Meanwhile, when Ravana heard about Rama and Sita's exile he realised that this was his chance for revenge. He lured Rama and Lakshmana away from Sita by sending a beautiful enchanted deer. When Rama and Lakshmana chased after the deer, Ravana kidnapped Sita and took her to his kingdom of Lanka.

In Lanka, Ravana tried to convince Sita to marry him, but she stayed true to Rama. Meanwhile, Rama joined forces with the monkey King, Sugreeva, who had also been exiled from his kingdom by his brother Bali. Rama helped Sugreeva to regain his kingdom and in return Sugreeva raised an army of monkeys and bears to help Rama rescue Sita. This army was led by the monkey god Hanuman.

Hanuman raced to Lanka, where he promised Sita that help would come soon. But on his way back he was captured and Ravana ordered his tail to be wrapped in oily rags and set on fire. Hanuman used his powers as a god to increase the length of his tail so much that there seemed no end to it. He escaped and used his burning tail to set fire to all of Lanka.

Meanwhile, Rama had gathered an army and had built a huge bridge between Lanka and the mainland. Rama and his army then crossed the ocean and destroyed Ravana's army. During the battle, Lakshmana was heavily wounded, but he was cured by a magic herb which Hanuman flew all the way to the Himalayas to obtain. Not finding the herb at first, Hanuman brought the entire mountain just to be sure. Finally, Rama and Sita were reunited and returned to Ayodhya to rule in peace.

This painting shows the end of the Ramayan when Rama and Hanuman fight a battle with the demon Ravenna and defeat him.

Decorations that show faith

Simple works of art and decorations are used to make people and gods feel welcome in temples and at home.

Rangoli

Many Hindus show their faith by decorating the entrances to their homes, workplaces and schools with special designs. Some people make the designs everyday, but many more use them during holy days and festivals. These designs are called rangoli or kolam.

Rangoli are used to make buildings look beautiful so they provide a welcome to gods, goddess and to ordinary people who come to visit.

Rangoli are drawn on the floor and made out of coloured powders, rice, flowers and chalk. There are no special designs, each person makes whatever design they would like.

A legend of rangoli

According to one legend, rangoli began long ago, when a king and his whole kingdom were mourning the death of the high priest's son. Everybody in the whole kingdom prayed to Lord Brahma. Lord Brahma was so moved by the prayers that he asked the king to paint a portrait of the boy on the floor. The king did this and Brahma breathed life into the painting and brought the boy back to life. And that is how rice, flour and flowers were made into offerings to God in the form of floor painting.

▶ To make a rangoli, the powdered colours are sprinkled on cleaned and dusted floors. The powder is usually applied 'freehand' by sprinkling it between the fingers.

▼ Statues decorated with garlands.

Garlands

Long strings of flowers, called garlands, are used as decoration to show acceptance and welcome. In temples, statues of gods and goddesses are decorated with garlands to show that the worshippers welcome the gods into the temple.

On special occasions, guests to homes or special events, such as festivals, may also be given garlands as a way to make them feel welcome.

Music for worship

Music used in Hindu worship does not usually use instruments.

Spoken or chanted prayers and songs are an important art that is used in everyday Hindu worship. The words of the prayers and songs help worshippers feel closer to the gods and to God. They also make it easier for the worshipper to think about God.

Hindu worship involves all of the senses and singing or chanting helps people to worship using the sense of hearing.

There are many kinds of prayers and songs used in worship. On these pages you can read about some that are used every day.

Mantras

Mantras are short prayers that are chanted. A mantra may be made up of a single syllable, like "Aum", a word or a short verse. Some people believe that repeating mantras over and over helps worshippers to feel calmer and closer to God. Here is an English version of one common mantra, called Mahamrityunjaya mantra:

> **We Meditate on God**
> Which moves through and nourishes all
>   like a fragrance.
> May we be freed from death to be with
>   God forever,
> Even as the cucumber is cut from bondage
>   to the creeper.

Shlokas

A shloka is a short prayer, a verse, phrase, proverb or hymn of praise. They are sung during worship. A shloka is usually made up of verses of two lines, with sixteen syllables each. Hindus recite shlokas before their daily rituals and during important events. Here is a part of a shloka. (Remember, the prayer is said in Sanskrit, so each verse may not be 16 syllables in English.)

> O Mother Earth, wearing oceans, forests
>   and mountains;
> Wife of Vishnu I bow to you. Forgive me
>   for placing my feet on you.
> On the front of the hand is Lakshmi,
>   Mother of prosperity,
> In the root of the hand is Saraswati,
>   Mother of learning.
> In the middle is Govinda (Krishna).
> Thus we respectfully see our hands in
>   the Morning.

Bhajans

Bhajans are simple songs, written in simple language, that tell of the worshippers love for God. Bhajans are often sung by a group of worshippers with a lead singer.

Bhajans might repeat words and phrases, or be chanted, to help the worshipper focus on God. The words may be popular sayings, stories from the lives of Gods, the preaching of Hindu saints and descriptions of God's glories.

Here are some short bhajans.

A bhajan to Krishna

Adoration to the Lord Vishnu, Shiva, who abides and shines in all beings and is one with Om Vishnu.

A bhajan to Lord Shiva

Bow to Parvati's Lord, Shiva, Supreme Lord Shiva, Bestower of Good and Destroyer of Evil, Unchanging Supreme Lord.

Bhajan to God

Although I don't see You, You are there. Although I can't touch You, You are there. Although I don't know You, You are Love. Although I don't understand You, You are wisdom in my heart. Thank You, Lord for letting me believe in You. Thank You, Lord, I know wherever I am You are, wherever I am You are.

Aarti

It is a Hindu tradition to end the worship service with a prayer song called an aarti. There are many aartis. Here is one that is used every day by many people, called Om Jaya Jagadeesh:

Oh Lord of the whole Universe
Mighty Lord of the whole Universe
All Thy devotees' agonies
All Thy devotees' sorrows
Instantly Thou banisheth
Oh Lord of the whole Universe

He who is immersed in devotion
He reaps the fruits of Thy love
Lord, he reaps the fruits of Thy love
Floating in a cloud of comforts
Floating in a cloud of comforts
Free from all the worldly problems
Oh Lord of the whole Universe

Thou art Mother and Father
At Thy feet I seek eternal truth
Lord, at Thy feet I seek eternal truth
There's none other than Thee, Lord
There's none other than Thee, Lord
Guardian of all our hopes
Oh Lord of the whole Universe

Thou art Godly perfection
Omnipotent Master of all
Lord, omnipotent Master of all
My destiny's in Thy Hand
My destiny's in Thy Hand
Supreme Soul of all Creation
Oh Lord of the whole Universe

Thou art an ocean of mercy
Gracious protector of all
Lord, gracious protector of all
I'm Thy humble devotee
I'm Thy humble devotee
Grant me Thy divine grace
Oh Lord of the whole Universe

Thou art beyond all perception
Formless and yet multiform
Lord, formless and yet multiform
Grant me a glimpse of Thyself
Grant me a glimpse of Thyself
Guide me along the path to Thee
Oh Lord of the whole Universe

Friend of the helpless and feeble
Benevolent saviour of all
Lord, benevolent saviour of all
Offer me Thy hand of compassion
Offer me Thy hand of compassion
I seek refuge at Thy feet
Oh Lord of the whole Universe

Surmounting the earthly desires
Free from the sins of this life
Lord, free from the sins of this life
Undivided faith and devotion
Undivided faith and devotion
In eternal service unto Thee
Oh Lord of the whole Universe

Oh Lord of the whole Universe
Mighty Lord of the whole Universe
All Thy devotees' agonies
All Thy devotees' sorrows
Instantly Thou banisheth
Oh Lord of the whole Universe

Art in everyday worship

Art is used by Hindus in every part of their daily worship.

This description of an ordinary day in the life of a Hindu in India shows how different types of art are used in everyday life and worship.

Ramachadran's day begins with his mother making a lotus design, using bleached rice flower, on the ground outside his family's door.

Ramachadran shaves and bathes, drinks tea and eats a rice cake. He then walks to the temple of the Goddess Mariamann, who conquers evil and heals disorder. He carries a wicker basket containing offerings of bananas and hibiscus flowers that he brought from home. On the way to the temple, Ramachadran also buys a coconut and incense from a street vendor.

As Ramachadran enters the temple he smells the incense. He hears worshippers chanting mantras and bhajans and he reaches up to ring a bell suspended from the ceiling. The sound of the bell clears his mind and helps him to focus on the deity. A priest collects his offerings.

As Ramachadran enters the shrine room a curtain is opened and he can see a beautiful statue of the goddess, dressed in a bright red sari and covered with garlands brought by the worshippers. The priest waves a brass lamp with seven flames in front of the goddess.

As Ramachandran looks at the statue, he sees and is seen by the goddess. He is filled with a feeling of well being, belonging and calmness. He feels that the goddess is in the statue, listening to his prayers.

▲ A tray of materials used in puja.

After singing aarti, the priest brings a tray of lighted camphor. The tray also contains ashes and red vermillion powder. Ramachadran waves his finger above the burning camphor and touches his eyelids. This stands for seeing God. He then puts his finger in the ashes and vermillion and touches his forehead.

These marks stand for purity and the power of God.

Before he leaves, the priest returns the baskets of bananas and coconuts to Ramachadran. The offerings have been blessed by the goddess during worship. Later Ramachadran's family will eat them and share the blessings. It makes Ramachadran feel good to know that the food has been blessed.

Ramachandran then returns home to prepare for his day at work as an engineer. Some days Ramachandran does not visit the temple but worships his goddess at his household shrine.

◀ This picture shows a statue from the temple Sri Mariymann in Singapore.

31

Index

Curriculum Visions

**There's much more on-line
including videos**

You will find multimedia resources covering
six different religions, as well as history,
geography, science and spelling subjects in
the subscription Professional Zone at:

www.CurriculumVisions.com

A CVP Book
Copyright Earthscape © 2008

Author
Lisa Magloff, MA

Senior Designer
Adele Humphries, BA

Editor
Gillian Gatehouse

Acknowledgements
The publishers would like to thank
everyone at the ISKCON Bhaktivendanta
Manor for their help and advice.

Photographs
The Earthscape Picture Library, except:
(c=centre, t=top, b=bottom, l=left, r=right)
DreamTime pages 24–25 (main), 24 (inset);
ShutterStock pages 2–3, 5r, 6, 7b, 8r, 9, 10tr,
12–13t, 13b, 15, 16 (main), 17 (inset), 18–19,
25 (inset), 30, 31bl; *TopFoto* pages 16 (inset),
17 (main), 20–21, 23.

Illustrations
David Woodroffe

Designed and produced by
Earthscape

Printed in China by
WKT Company Ltd

Hindu art and writing
– Curriculum Visions
**A CIP record for this book is
available from the British Library**
ISBN: 978 1 86214 248 0

*This product is manufactured from
sustainable managed forests. For every tree
cut down at least one more is planted.*